Contents

What is a bear?

Bears are mammals. They are related to dogs and wolves. Most bears are large animals with big heads, small round ears and little forward-facing eyes. Their large bodies are supported by short, strong legs armed with powerful claws.

X-Ray Vision

Hold the page opposite up to the light and see what's inside a polar bear.

See what's inside

Mammals are warm-blooded and keep their body at a constant high temperature. They have fur or hair that keeps them warm. Bears are warm-blooded and covered in fur – they are mammals.

Is a bear a mammal?

Yes, a bear is a mammal.

Is a bird a mammal?

No, a bird is not a mammal.

Birds are also warm-blooded but they have feathers instead of fur.

Scary Creatures
BEARS

Written by
Gerald Legg

Illustrated by
Mark Bergin

Created and designed
by David Salariya

BOOK HOUSE

Author:

Dr Gerald Legg holds a doctorate in zoology from Manchester University. He worked in West Africa for several years as a lecturer and rainforest researcher. His current position is biologist at the Booth Museum of Natural History in Brighton.

Artist:

Mark Bergin was born in Hastings in 1961. He studied at Eastbourne College of Art and has illustrated many children's non-fiction books. He lives in Bexhill-on-Sea with his wife and three children.

Series creator:

David Salariya was born in Dundee, Scotland. In 1989 he established The Salariya Book Company. He has illustrated a wide range of books and has created many new series for publishers in the UK and overseas. He lives in Brighton with his wife, illustrator Shirley Willis, and their son.

Cover Artist:

Carolyn Scrace

Editors:

Stephanie Cole
Karen Barker Smith

Photographic credits:

Published in Great Britain in 2002 by Book House, an imprint of
The Salariya Book Company Ltd
25 Marlborough Place, Brighton BN1 1UB

Visit the Salariya Book Company at:
www.salariya.com
www.book-house.co.uk

ISBN 1 904194 29 X

A catalogue record for this book is available from the British Library.

Printed and bound in Italy.

Printed on paper from sustainable forests.

powerful jaws

big paws

claws

thick fur

strong legs

5

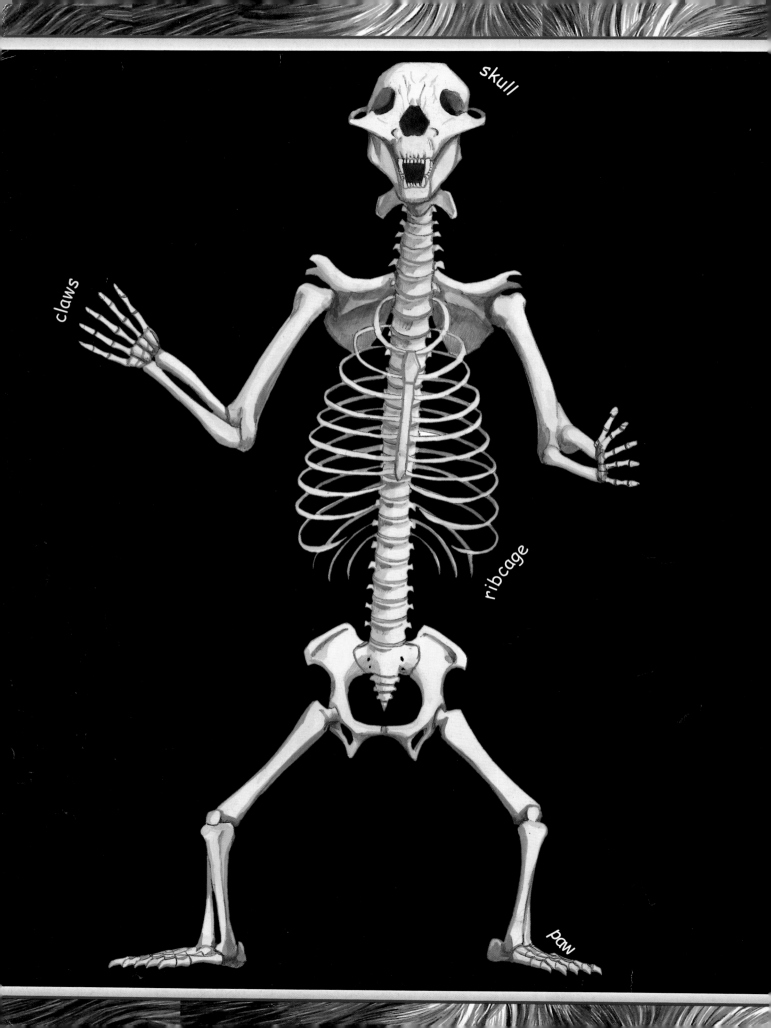

What is inside a bear?

Bears, like all mammals, have a bony skeleton. The head and skull are supported by a neck that is part of the backbone. The backbone ends in a short tail.

A wide, strong ribcage protects the lungs, heart, liver and other organs. Bears' paws are very big and have five toes that end in sharp claws.

The skeleton of a bear allows it to stand upright, like people do.

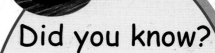

Did you know?

Our cuddly teddy bears are modelled on the brown bear. They are named after an American President, Theodore Roosevelt, who refused to shoot a cub on a hunting trip in 1902.

A bear skull

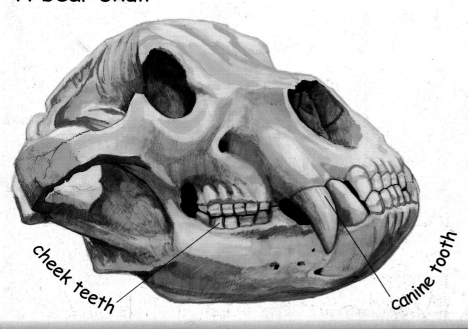

cheek teeth

canine tooth

Bears have very strong skulls (left). Huge jaw muscles are attached to the skull. These make the bear's head very big. Bears have sharp canine teeth and broad, flat cheek teeth. This means that they can eat any type of food they like.

Why are bears scary?

Bears are big, very strong, clever and bad-tempered. They can easily kill other animals and people with their powerful claws and teeth. It is easy to accidentally get close to a bear and this can frighten it into attacking without warning. Most bears are scared of people, so making plenty of noise will keep them away.

Did you know?

If a bear sees you and lowers its head this is a sign that it is about to attack. Don't crouch down or the bear will think you are about to attack too!

Which bear is the scariest?

American brown bears (including grizzly bears) are amongst the largest living land carnivores. They can weigh up to 850 kg and stand over 2.8 m tall making them very scary. They will not hesitate to attack. Polar bears are the most aggressive bears of all. They are not frightened of anything!

Brown bears and polar bears are the scariest!

A fierce brown bear growling

Standing tall, this large brown bear opens its mouth and growls a warning to other bears. He is protecting his territory and letting other bears know that he is in charge.

What do bears eat?

Bears will eat just about anything, including small mammals, insects, carrion, fruit, grass, roots, leaves and even people's rubbish.

A bear uses its front paws as eating tools. Their sharp claws can catch and hold prey, tear trees open to look for insects, dig for roots and grubs, rip flesh and even catch fish.

Giant panda eating bamboo

Did you know?

Sun bears are very noisy eaters. They make a noise so loud that it can be heard several kilometres away.

Giant pandas (left) spend 10 to 12 hours a day eating about 14 kg of their favourite food, bamboo. They can eat up to 40% of their body weight! Sometimes they eat other plants and occasionally small mammals and fish.

Polar bears like to eat seals. They sniff out baby seals that hide in the snow and wait patiently for them to come out of their breathing holes in the ice.

In summer, polar bears eat fish, birds, eggs and some plants. They will also eat any dead walruses and whales that they find. Polar bears eat more meat than any other type of bear.

Polar bear eating an eider duck

Where do bears live?

Polar bears live in the Arctic regions. Other bears are found in either the tropical forests of India, Sri Lanka and Southeast Asia, or the mountains of South America. They also live in the temperate forests of Southeast Asia, Europe and North America.

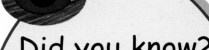

Did you know?

In Britain, as in many parts of the world, bears have been hunted into extinction. They were last seen in Britain 1200 years ago.

Polar bears (below) have to walk huge distances across the Arctic ice in search of food. Food is very hard to find in these surroundings.

Polar bear walking across the Arctic ice

Brown bears live in temperate forests, but they can also live in other areas like open plains, tundra and subalpine mountain areas of North America, Europe, Japan and North Asia. They used to live throughout Europe and North America, but there are fewer of them now because of hunting and the loss of their habitats.

own bear in the mountains of North America

Are bears good hunters?

Most bears are very good hunters. The polar bear is the best. It is very patient and can sneak up on its prey quietly. Brown bears hunt small mammals and attack deer, moose and even young buffalo.

A brown bear showing its big teeth

Smaller bears also hunt small mammals, fish, birds and insects.

Did you know?

Brown bears living on the islands of Kodiak and Admiralty in Alaska are the largest land carnivores in the world. They are up to a third larger than their mainland cousins.

Brown bears hunting for fish

How do bears catch fish?

Brown bears are excellent at fishing (above). When the salmon are swimming up-stream they catch the fish with their paws or even snatch them with their mouths as the fish leap the rapids. Bears can grow very fat and large on this rich diet.

Bears catch fish with their teeth and their claws!

Did you know?

Grasshoppers, crickets, beetles and caterpillars are favourite foods of American black bears. These, finished off with some honey, acorns, blueberries and mountain holly make a fine meal.

Is a panda a bear?

Yes, a panda is a bear. Until 1995, scientists thought the giant panda was a member of the raccoon family rather than a bear.

The giant panda is almost dependant on one type of food, bamboo. To crush this tough plant, pandas have powerful jaw muscles and special flattened cheek teeth. Bamboo naturally dies off every few years making it difficult for pandas to find food. This, together with habitat loss and poaching, has reduced their numbers to about one thousand.

Panda paw

extra sixth toe

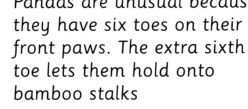

Pandas are unusual because they have six toes on their front paws. The extra sixth toe lets them hold onto bamboo stalks

Giant pandas in China

 Did you know?

When first born a baby bear is tiny. A baby panda is the smallest of all the bear species, weighing only 80-140 g.

A panda's diet is almost entirely made up of bamboo shoots and bamboo roots. They also eat other plants including iris and crocus bulbs, grasses and occasionally fish, insects and small rodents.

Are bears good parents?

A female bear has to be a very good parent as the males have nothing to do with raising the cubs. The mother bear keeps her tiny, newborn cubs warm with her long fur. She also teaches her cubs what to eat, how to find food and how to catch prey.

X-Ray Vision

Hold the page opposite up to the light and see what's inside a pregnant bear.

See what's inside

Polar bear with cubs

Did you know?

If a polar bear cub is in difficulty swimming, its mother will rescue it by grabbing its leg. Black bears send their cubs up a tree if there is danger and sloth bears carry their cubs away from danger on their backs.

A pregnant brown bear

powerful shoulder muscle

ribs

lung

developing cubs

20

When do cubs leave their parents?

Newborn cubs stay with their mother in their den until early spring. The larger bears such as the polar, black and brown bears, suckle their cubs until they weigh about 2 kg.

Learning about their new world takes time, so most cubs stay with their mother for at least two years. Then they are on their own. They start their own family four to seven years later.

Brown bear suckling cubs

Sows (female bears) usually suckle their cubs laying on their back or on their side.

What do bears do in summer and in winter?

In summer, life is easy for most bears. In the spring, plants begin to grow and produce leaves, shoots, flowers and fruits. Other small animals come out of their winter hiding places. Bears have plenty to eat.

Did you know?

Some female bears, like the brown bear, mate with more than one male. This leads to the cubs in one litter having different fathers.

Brown bear cubs are born in the winter. In the summer they can explore their new world with their mother and grow strong. It is a time to relax, explore, play and eat.

Brown bear cubs playing

For many bears winters are cold and food is hard to find, so they find a safe, sheltered cave or hollow tree in which to sleep. This is not really hibernation because their body temperature and heart rate stay the same. The temperature of true hibernators falls close to that of their surroundings and their heart rate slows down.

Female bears also spend time in the winter looking after and feeding their newborn cubs.

Did you know?

A bear can sleep for several months in its den, living off the fat it puts on during the summer. It may lose 15%-40% of its body weight just by sleeping.

When winter starts, the female polar bear digs her den in the snow and sleeps (right). In late November or early December she gives birth to twins. She is a good mother and she stays with the cubs for weeks without eating anything.

A polar bear and her cubs in the den

Why are polar bears white?

The polar bear's white fur is very important. It camouflages the polar bear as it hunts its prey across the snow and ice or waits in hiding for animals to come out of their shelters.

The polar bear's white fur also protects a layer of warm yellow wool. Furry soles protect the polar bear's feet against the cold and help them grip the ice.

Polar bear

Did you know?

Although they look white, polar bears have black skin and a black tongue and nose to trap heat. The white fur is actually translucent and lets the warming sunlight through to the black skin where it can be absorbed.

Do polar bears get cold?

Beneath the polar bear's skin there is a thick layer of fat. This, together with a warm coat of fur, keeps a polar bear warm even in the coldest weather, when temperatures can get as low as -40°C.

Did you know?
Despite their size, polar bears are very fast runners. They can out-run a reindeer over short distances and swim at 4 kph.

No, polar bears never get cold.

Polar bear in the snow

Bears around the world

Polar bears are the largest of all the bears. They are found in the Arctic regions.

Brown bears are found in more parts of the world than any other bear. They live throughout the cool northern forests of America, Europe, Japan and North Asia.

Bears live all around the world from tropical forests to the icy Arctic. Bears have never lived in Africa, though, except for in the Atlas mountains.

Polar bear

Brown bear

American black bear

About 750,000 black bears live in North America.

The spectacled bear is found in the forested mountain areas of South America.

Spectacled bear

Pandas are now only found in small regions of southwest China, living in an area covering about 13,800 square km. They live in the mountainside bamboo forests.

Brown bear

Panda

Asiatic black bear

Asiatic black bears are found throughout hilly, forested areas of Southern Asia.

Sloth bear

Sun bear

Sloth bears live in the the forests and grasslands of India and surrounding countries.

The sun bear is the smallest type of bear, weighing about 100 kg. It is found in the tropical rainforests of Southeast Asia.

What are bears scared of?

Bears have very few enemies. Most bears die from accidents and diseases. However, thousands of bears are shot for 'sport' in North America every year, making humans their worst enemy.

Many bears are kept in captivity, often in poor conditions, so that they can be used to entertain people and make money.

A sun bear caged in Taiwan

Bears are very intelligent animals and can be trained very easily when they are young. This often means that the mother is killed so that her cub can be kept.

Training is often cruel and bears hate to be kept in small spaces and cages.

Did you know?

In Asia, bears are killed and used in traditional medicine. Sloth bears are caught and caged. They have a tube stuck into their gall bladder so their bile can be milked and sold.

Did you know?

Six of the eight species of bears are nearly extinct. Even the other two, the brown bear and American black bear, are under threat. We do not know how many of some species are still alive but there are less than a thousand spectacled bears.

This Asiatic black bear is performing in New Delhi, India (right). In many parts of the world it is illegal to use animals in this way.

A performing black bear

Bears facts

Brown bears can tear open a locked freezer to get at the food inside.

Spectacled bears will climb cacti to taste the sweet fruit at the top.

The fur of black bears used to be made into the bearskin hats worn by British guardsman soldiers. Only fake fur is used today.

Brown bears have an extremely good sense of smell. The part of the nose that is used to pick up scent is 100 times bigger in a bear than in a person.

Black bears are not always black. They can be brown, white and even blue!

People often make the mistake of thinking that the koala is a bear. The koala is in fact closely related to the kangaroo and is not a bear at all.

Spectacled bears build themselves platforms out of branches in the treetops. They use these platforms as places to feed and sleep.

Female bears are called sows and males are called boars.

The sloth bear's diet is made up of almost nothing but termites. It can make its muzzle into a tube shape and use it to suck termites from their nest.

The polar bear's front paws are webbed like a duck's. This makes them very good swimmers.

Polar bears have a second, clear eyelid. It protects their eyes while they are swimming, like built-in goggles.

Sun bears have no hair on the palms of their paws. This makes it easier for them to hold on to the trees they climb.

 # Glossary

bile A green, bitter liquid produced by the liver as waste and used to help to digest fats.

canine teeth The two pointed teeth on either side at the front of the jaws.

carnivore An animal that hunts and kills other animals for food.

carrion The rotting flesh of a dead animal.

cheek teeth The teeth in the sides of the jaw used for crushing and chewing.

extinction When a species of plant or animal is no longer alive.

gall bladder The bag-like sac that collects and stores bile from the liver.

habitat An animal's natural surroundings and living place.

hibernation When animals spend the winter months sleeping in a nest or shelter. An animal's breathing and heart rate slow down when they are hibernating.

muzzle The part of a bear's face that sticks out and forms the nose and jaw.

poaching Illegally hunting animals.

prey Animals hunted and killed by other animals, called predators, for food.

raccoon A badger-like carnivore that lives in North America.

rapids Fast flowing part of a river where the water rushes over rocks.

sow The name for a female bear.

subalpine The parts of mountains below the cold rocky area, but above where trees grow.

suckle To suck and drink milk from a mother.

temperate The parts of the world that have a warm or hot summer and a cool or cold winter.

translucent Almost see-through.

tropical The parts of the world where it is usually hot all the year round.

tundra The cold desert north of the Arctic circle where few plants grow.

warm-blooded An animal whose temperature remains almost the same, whatever the temperature around it.

Index